Published by
Sungold Editions
Santa Barbara

ISBN: 978-0-9991678-5-4

GETTING TO KNOW
MY BROTHER'S KILLER

DOCUMENTARY POEMS

BY TOM HUTH

Sungold Editions
2021

CONTENTS

BUS
RIDE
HOME

Across the snowdusted plains of Nebraska
grasslands cloaked in deadwinter gray
the trees but ghosts of trees

Easing through towns in the evening
cones of lamplight in the windows
beacons of kinship and warmth

North Platte
    Grand Island
        Lincoln
Going back to Detroit
    to sit in vigil
        with my mother
Council Bluffs
    Cedar Rapids
        Davenport

What could have happened to my brother
on a business trip to San Francisco
except that fate we cannot accept?

Mom hopes Jerry was hit on the head
and is wandering around with amnesia
I hope he staged the disappearance
to ditch his corporate job
and his domineering wife
    and even his children
if that's what it took to be free

MOTOR
CITY

The bus pulls into the station
MOTOWN the baggage handler calls
BRING THAT BUCKET ON OVER HERE

Mom in her tidy blue raincoat
    I'm glad you're here honey
She doesn't usually call me that
    The car's just a block away

We walk the broken sidewalks
Are you still driving the Olds?
    Gosh it has only 60,000 miles
a safe Detroit conversation

When she takes out her keys
she glances into the back seat
    What does she know?
    Was that how it happened?
A man was hiding in Jerry's car?
put an arm around his neck?
    a gun to his head?

She asks me to lock my door
    Was that how it happened?
He jumped into Jerry's car
    at a red light?

She reminds me to buckle up
    and I do

THE
TELEPHONE

Day after day we sit in her condo
playing Scrabble
    an old comfort of ours
waiting for the phone to ring

If she runs an errand I tag along
so I won't be alone with the phone
    and have to give her the news
when she walks in the door

One night we go to the race track
and she cheers for my horses
    with that girlish gaiety
she's always been able to muster

Then we have to go home
and I dread when she puts
    the key in the door
because the phone is inside

Taking
Our
Medicine

On Sunday evening we sip
Manhattans an old comfort
and watch the local news
    nothing but murders

We admit it would be better
for that phone call to come
than to never ever find out

Then at midnight it comes
She gets it in her bedroom
I pick up in the kitchen
Jerry's wife Sue
    Well they found him
    way down the coast
    in a farmer's field
    shot in the temple

She says the escaped convict
who did it was captured
in Arizona after killing
three more travelers there

But we aren't the kind of people
who'd jump up in a courtroom
    and cry out for revenge
We know how to take our medicine
That's Mom's Midwestern strength
    and my strength too

A
PLEDGE

I walk back
to her room

longest
 walk
  of
   my
    life

She's perched
on the edge
of the bed
weeping

I sit down
put my arm
around her
cry with her
cry for her

She turns her
flooded eyes to me
     Please don't let
     anything happen
     to you honey

Me the carefree son
I won't Mom
I promise

15

THE
FUNERAL

A suburb of Minneapolis
my first time in Jerry's house
his absence spooking every room
I hardly know his teen-aged kids
a girl and two younger brothers
        I never did like Sue
        how she treated Jerry

The service is Saturday morning
at her Christian Science church
        the casket closed

The minister mispronounces
our name and I'm incensed
How dare you disgrace Jerry!
You didn't even know him!
        But I keep my peace
I didn't know Jerry either

Later I drive Mom to the airport
her only defense now to move on
After she was widowed at 47
she invented a brave new life
career culture world travel
        Now at 65 she has more
                memories to entomb

BACK
ON
THE
BUS

As the northern sun goes down
I board a westbound Trailways
for Sioux Falls and Denver

St. Peter
    Mankato
        Worthington
piecing together
    the few crumbs
        of evidence

Jerry was last seen leaving
work at 6 p.m. on a Tuesday

The next morning his Hertz car
was abandoned in the East Bay
with a bashed left front fender
400 extra miles on the odometer
and blood on the passenger seat

Detectives checked Jerry's room
at the Bay Bridge Holiday Inn
his bed unslept in
    his belongings untouched

Eleven days later
his body was found
200 miles to the south

Passengers
of
the
Night

The conclusion is inescapable
    the image indelible
Jerry and his murderer
must have ridden together
for hours sitting side by side
    staring out the windshield
        at the onrushing night

until Jerry
met his end

As a brother as a journalist
I hunger to know what happened
that evening on the highways
of central California

    What did they talk about?
    Did they make any stops?
    Did Jerry try to escape?
    Did he ever have a chance?
    What was it like for him
    the most gripping encounter
        of his 39 years?

I would like to believe
my brother's final night
was not some horror show
but a drama more complex

An
Investigation

Jerry was the older brother
    the cautious one
quiet serious better behaved
We grew up sharing a bedroom
but never learned how to be
allies sidekicks confidantes
    He built model boats
    I was the funny kid

As adults we lived far apart
and saw each other only back
in Detroit for the holidays
Then I left my job and family
and dropped out to Colorado
Sue made me the black sheep
I didn't see my only brother
    for his last seven years

At least I can try to learn
how he spent his last hours

Four years after the crime
I fly out to San Francisco
to discover how Jerry died
and maybe learn a little
    about how he lived

THE
POLICE
REPORTS

The officer behind the desk
hands across a thick folder
tabbed HUTH GERALD OWEN
She confides
    Some cases affect you
    more than others
    the family and all

The initial reports
written in the field
are dry and procedural
and instantly riveting

At 9:45 a.m. on January 16 a man
hereinafter known as the Suspect
came into the Mobil Gas Station
at 97 Abbott Street and said
his vehicle had run out of gas

A white male 35-36 years old
5'11" 140 pounds very thin
sunken cheeks pale complexion
and carrying a large amount
of United States currency

When the tow-truck driver brought
the car into the station he advised
the manager of suspicious contents
a bedsheet heavily stained by blood

JERRY'S
ROOM

Here is what detectives
found in the hotel room
Jerry never returned to

Slacks and a Western shirt
laid out for the evening
        more organized than me
In the dresser jockey shorts
        whereas I wear briefs

A fastidious traveler
shoe polish nail clippers
hair spray a hair dryer
Maybe Sue did his packing
Is it wrong to spy on him?

On top of the dresser
a classified ad from
the Sunday Chronicle
circled in red ink

        7 Beauties Companions
        Your Place Is Fine
        We've Got the Time

CITY
LIGHTS

I drive my Hertz rental
to the Bay Bridge Holiday Inn
and ask to look at Room 624

What is there to see?
the bed where he lay
the dresser the desk
the toilet the sink
a cell like any other
the window sealed shut
to discourage jumpers

I am saddened to note
that Jerry's last view
was not of the spires
of San Francisco but
the sprawl of Oakland

And he would have been
the last person to ask
      for a better room

IN THEIR TRACKS

Driving down from San Francisco
    retracing their route on the 101
past freight yards and shipping docks
past office parks abandoned to the moon
past shapely groves of eucalyptus trees
past cherry stands closed for the season
through the Salinas Valley they drove
    heading south

Did Jerry tell Donald Harding about
his job? his children? his hopes?
Did he believe he would survive?
Did he imagine returning home
    with an unbelievable tale?

I case out the motel room
they checked into at 12:03 a.m.
    (the bloody bedsheet)

I stand upon the very soil
in a fallow field nearby
where Jerry was found lying
covered by his sport jacket
as if in some final gesture
of compassion or condolence

Still the detective was right
There's only one way to know
    how that night went down

DEAR MR. HARDING

I am the brother of Jerry Huth
whom you've admitted to killing
near Paso Robles California

First let me explain that I
bear no ill will toward you
I am writing merely to ask
how that evening played out
and how Jerry lost his life

I would like to know
How did you come upon Jerry?
What happened on that ride?
What did you two talk about?
Did you use your first names?
Did you stop along the way?
    Was he tied up?
    Was he afraid?
Did he ever try to get away?
Tell me what happened
    at the Black Oak Motor Lodge
Did Jerry sleep before he died?
    And why did you kill him?

Thank you

I'll be waiting
for your reply

EASY
PICKINS

Jerry's murderer
has my address now

He has a long history
of escaping from jail

Arizona's penitentiary
is a day's drive away

Our small mountain town
is a good place to hide

He would see me
as sympathetic

He would think
*Those Huth boys
are easy pickins*

FROM
DEATH
ROW

I walk down to our mailbox
to find a business envelope
from the Arizona State Prison
with a bulky object inside

I stare at the lettering
at Donald Harding's handwriting
    so practiced so precise
block letters of equal size and spacing
like my dad's hand in old photo albums
Here is one thing Harding cares about

I stand fingering the envelope
    picture him in his cell
        licking these stamps
What is wrong with me
    that I want to recognize
        his humanity?

I peel it open in the driveway
careful to preserve the writing
Inside a cassette tape labeled
    APPROX 45 MINS DISCUSSION

First thing next morning
I walk out to my office
sit down with a coffee
push in the cassette
    and press PLAY

HIS
VOICE

Metallic noises
Two men shouting
TEN-FIFTY!
    WHAT?
ON YOUR FEET!

A grainy silence

Then a soft voice
chillingly intimate
right by my side

Tom?
Don Harding here

It's Sunday night just before eleven
I'm sorry I haven't responded sooner
I've been away on some legal matters
trying to block my pending execution

I have waited until things
quieted down in the cellblock
It gets pretty noisy in here
hard to collect your thoughts

For the moment there's a lull
I don't know if it will last
but let me try to give you
what you're looking for

Confinement

I've been in confinement all my life
and I'm not telling you this Tom
to solicit sympathy or forgiveness
I just want to give you a picture
of the person who's responsible
for your brother's death okay?

What a shock: polite temperate
reasonable lucid articulate

I've been in confinement since I was
sent to reform school when I was ten
because I kept running away from home
But I ran away from reform school too
so when I was fifteen they sent me
to the Arkansas State Penitentiary

It is important I tell you this Tom
It was a very brutal very hard place
this country's most notorious prison
I will gladly spare you the details
but I went there when I was a child
    and I grew up there
and I think that was responsible
    more than anything
for putting into motion
the forces of destruction
that climaxed in your brother's death
and the deaths of several other people

BAD
COMPANY

I got paroled when I was twenty-four
but I could not adjust to society
I could only relate to ex-convicts

One night I got into a fight in a bar
and got sent back to the penitentiary
After four years they let me out again
but I was drawn into that same circle
ex-convicts the only people I knew

I got into a fight at a party
The guy fired a shot at me
I picked up a kitchen knife
and stabbed him
and he died

But I broke out of jail
     and that began the motion
          that led to the death
               of all those people

A
Dark
Parking
Lot

I met Jerry outside his hotel
I was feeling extreme paranoia
a fear of being recaptured
just going from state to state
on a blind destructive course
trying to retain my freedom
and I went through
     a lot of stuff
before the night I met Jerry

It was outside a Holiday Inn
I was looking for anyone
who appeared to have money
I was flat broke
had no transportation
and I seen him park
in the parking lot
a dark parking lot

I approached him
and introduced myself
as a security guard
I showed him an ID
and a fictitious badge
and got him to relax

     Then I said
Get back in the car
This is a robbery

CASHING CHECKS

I told Jerry to drive
and we took the freeway south

I explained that I was on the run
that I was desperate
that I planned to take his car
    and his money
and leave him tied up somewhere

I wanted him to see that
I was in a rational state
I didn't want him to fear
I was some kind of maniac
and you may be thinking
that's exactly what I am
        I don't know
            I've changed
            so much

Jerry had hardly any cash
but he had travelers' checks
and he was more than willin'
    to cash them

So we stopped at hamburger places
    two or three of them
and ordered coffee or whatever
    just to cash checks

TALKING
RELIGION

It was pretty relaxed in the car
    considering the circumstances
We talked about his family
    his hobbies his likes
He was an electronic engineer
    in Minnesota he told me

He showed me a photograph
of his family on a sailboat
his wife and three children

We talked about religion
how we were both agnostics

Jerry was curious to understand
how I ended up in this situation
so I related quite a bit of my life
my confinement and what led to this

I told him I was sorry it was him
that he was a likeable person
    and he was Tom

I called him Jerry
    He called me Don
        We were makin' the best
            of a bad situation

THE
BLACK
OAK
MOTOR
LODGE

Around midnight we stopped at a motel
I rented a room and used the sheets
to tie him to the bedposts
     then I left

     Or I pretended to leave
     to see if he'd try to escape
because sometimes when I tied people up
they got loose and called the police
and I made lots of narrow getaways

     I stood outside behind a bush
     and watched through the window
     and sure enough I saw Jerry
     freeing himself from his bonds

So I went back into the room
and told him I'd have to find
some woods and tie him to a tree
I knew he'd be miserable as hell
I said Jerry I'm afraid you'll
     have to rough it out there

He turned to me and said
     If you're going to kill me
     shoot me between the eyes
I assured him I would not harm him
But something between us had changed
He didn't trust the situation anymore

FATAL
RECOURSE

We got back
on the freeway

I was driving
looking for some
isolated woods

Jerry's hands were tied
behind his back
and he uhhhhhhhhhhhh
      he kicked me

The car nearly wrecked
It skidded and swerved
and hit the guard rail
      and I shot him

It was an impulsive reaction
He didn't know what hit him

So I can tell you Tom that
your brother died bravely
      trying to escape

He never at any point
cowered you know

      Silently I thank him
      for telling us that

REMORSE

Finally I want to tell you Tom
that I am very sorry
from the bottom of my heart
that I took your brother's life
    in the prime of his life

I'm sorry for the grief
it has caused you
and your family
    his mother
    his wife
    his children
I'm very sorry

If
 if I could
  if my death could
   if it could restore
    all of those lives
I would die in peace

I don't know

Okay Jerry
I mean Tom
Take care

Bye

SAILOR BOY

I know the photograph
of the sailboat Jerry
showed to Don Harding
It hangs on Mom's wall

As a teen-ager Jerry
captained toy boats
around suburban lakes
by remote control
both of us such loners

As a man he captained
his own sailboat around
the waters of Minnesota
He would have been glad
to show me the ropes
        if I'd ever visited

Jerry took his family
on sailing trips abroad
Fiji and the Caribbean
but I heard about them
only from our mother

        Did Don Harding get
        to know Jerry better
        in six hours than I
        did in a lifetime?

WHO
WANTS
TO
KNOW?

I phone Mom in Detroit

I found out how Jerry died
and it wasn't as terrible
as we might have feared
Would you like to know?
It might ease your mind

She replies quietly evenly
without hesitation
      No thank you honey

I reach out to Jerry's widow
She is mortified I would ask

      I don't understand
Won't the truth free them from
the black hole of imagination?

My righteousness blinds me
to the depths of their pain
Over the years I ask Jerry's
grown children if they want
to know how their dad died

It only drives them away
      Uncle Tom a scary guy

THE
GAS
CHAMBER

The teaching is biblical
Don Harding can do unto others
only as others have done unto him
    capture them and confine them

After 13 years of appeals
his execution is scheduled
for what would have been
    Jerry's 52nd birthday

His mother Maycle comes from Arkansas
    to say good-bye
His older brother Darryl comes
    the son who turned out good

At midnight Don is led to his destiny
    wearing nothing but underpants
Witnesses hear shouting and stomping
    welling up from the cellblocks

He is strapped into the chair
spots Arizona's attorney general
    gives him the finger

At 18 minutes 29 seconds after midnight
as death-penalty opponents pray outside
and locals celebrate with firecrackers
    a lever is pulled dropping cyanide
    into a solution of sulfuric acid

ULTIMATE CONFINEMENT

The prisoner breathes deeply
A white cloud of gas rises
above his bare shoulders
He tilts his head back
rolls it side to side
Tremors run through
nerves and muscles
like bugs racing
under his skin
He convulses
He gasps

The torture goes on
for eleven minutes
before a doctor studying
an electrocardiograph
pronounces him dead

Laments the attorney general
    It was horrible to watch
    It took so long
Pronounces a TV anchorman
    We put animals to death
    more humanely than that

Jerry was granted 39 good years
By grace he perished instantly
Don Harding died as he lived
all struggle and suffering

www.ingramcontent.com/pod-product-compliance
Lightning Source LLC
Chambersburg PA
CBHW010247030426
42336CB00022B/3325